What Are You Learning?

cut

count

write

draw

wait

share

listen

read

What are you learning?

I'm learning to count.

What are you learning?

I'm learning to wait.

What are you learning?

I'm learning
to draw.

What are you learning?

I'm learning to cut.

What are you learning?

I'm learning to share.

What are you learning?

I'm learning to read.

Let's learn more about Spain.

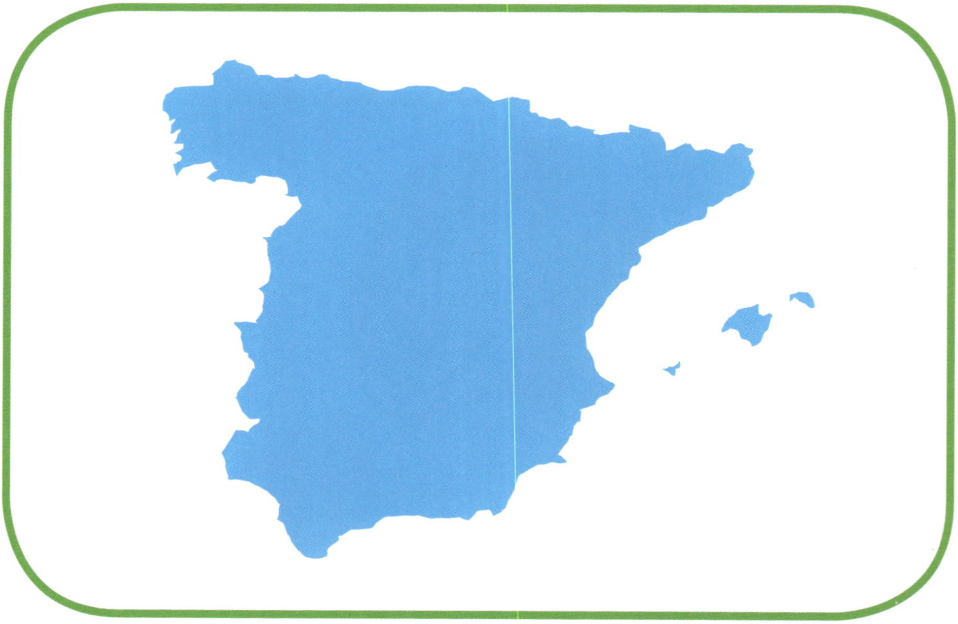

Paella